A

Case

for

Infant Baptism

by

Colin Buchanan

Honorary Assistant Bishop, Diocese of Rochester
Member of the Church of England Doctrine Commission

GROVE BOOKS LIMITED
Bramcote   Nottingham   NG9 3DS

CONTENTS

Copyright Colin Buchanan 1973, 1978, 1984 and 1989

INTRODUCTORY NOTE TO FOURTH EDITION

In 1972 I wrote one of the earliest of Grove Booklets – Ministry and Worship no. 3, *Baptismal Discipline.* In the course of it I summarised some headings which point to the rightness of baptising infants from Christian families, and from then on I was looking for a chance to write this 'case' for infant baptism. It has proved very popular, and now reaches its fourth edition. In the meantime I have written a series of further booklets: no. 24 (in tandem with David Pawson) *Infant Baptism under Cross-Examination,* no. 61 *One Baptism Once* (recently reprinted), no. 65 *Liturgy for Initiation: The Series 3 Services,* no. 91 *Adult Baptisms,* no. 98 *Policies for Infant Baptism* (replacing the previous no. 3), and Liturgical Study no. 48 *Anglican Confirmation.* I have tried to do little with this 'Case' over the years, partly because the other booklets cross-refer to it, partly because life has been too busy for radical re-writing, and in general I have seen no reason to want to change the case to-day. I have slightly updated the original Introduction opposite. I have deleted 'Postscripts' added for the second and third editions and have now written a new one (page 32). And I have tried to keep the footnoted references up to date also.

My hopes of writing 'a bigger and more scholarly work' were never realized, but at last others who share my biblical stance are producing fuller volumes relating to infant baptism – notably Michael 8reen (*Baptism,* Hodder, 1987) and Gordon Kuhrt (*Believing in Baptism,* Mowbray, 1987). So now I may never try to do it. I have found myself instead occupying the role of President of the Movement for the Reform of Infant Baptism (MORIB). It is a good position from which to distinguish oneself from both the anti-pedobaptists on the one hand, and the indiscriminate baptisers of infants on the other.

COB   24 November 1989

THE COVER PICTURE
is by Peter Ashton

First Edition October 1973
Second Edition August 1978
Third Edition April 1984
Fourth Edition (by Grove Books Limited) January 1990

ISSN 0305-3067
ISBN 1 85174 131 3

INTRODUCTION

The need for the 'case' for infant baptism to be made is obvious. What is not so obvious is what the case is *opposing*. The treatment here is designed to oppose solely the case that there is no such thing as infant baptism. This case I have abruptly dubbed the 'Baptist' position, though I am well aware that there are many Baptists who acknowledge the propriety (even if coupled with the undesirability) of infant baptism. Equally there are many who do not call themselves Baptists who seem to oppose infant baptism. Thus, with this apology, the terms 'pedobaptist' (i.e. those who approve, or at least allow, infant baptism) and 'Baptist' are used here to save long explanations at each stage. And it must be laboured that the case is only made against the Baptist *who is one in this sense.* Where Christians can agree that infant baptism *is* Christian baptism, even whilst differing about its desirability in any, or all, cases, then there is much less of a head-on meeting than is envisaged in the following pages.

I am also concerned not to make a wrongly-grounded case (which is to play into one's opponents' hands). Pedobaptists will themselves find some of their slicker arguments here repudiated. In particular, I would disavow any pedobaptist position which relied mainly upon any of:—authorities other than Scripture, arguments which would lead to indiscriminate baptism, theologies which make infant baptism different in kind from adult baptism, a devaluation of regeneration, a divorce between baptism and the beginning of the overt Christian life, an automatic efficacy in baptism, or a misapplication of the concept of the covenant.

This booklet's arguments lie behind those of nos. 3 and 98 in the series, (s ee Introductory note opposite). Setting out the arguments raises further problems – one is that further arguments about the nature of baptism itself lie behind this booklet, but cannot be deployed here. Another is that the treatment of infant baptism here is itself limited by space. An instance of this is the impossibility of dealing with the disparate views and arguments of a host of writers. I have a fair acquaintance with the field, but I find firstly that the best Baptist statement is in an unprinted syllabus (from around 1960) by Paul King Jewett, and secondly that the pedobaptist case has gone by default in recent years in terms of refuting not only Jewett, but also Beasley-Murray, White, Barth, Gilmore, Warns, Watson, Carson and even Dunn. For both these reasons it has been necessary at intervals to lay out arguments on both sides without attribution of sources. Those who know the authors will recognize the sources.[1]

There is obviously need for a bigger and more scholarly work, and I hope one day to write it. Meanwhile, like an architect at an intermediate stage of designing, I offer this working-drawing of the finished building. I am fairly confident it will stand up, but I am quite ready for small adjustments.

I must acknowledge help from many, particularly my own students, the Group for Renewal of Worship (GROW) and the Tyndale New Testament Studies Group before whom I find myself reading some of this material at ten-year intervals over against my good friend David Pawson. But it will be obvious that the booklet expresses my thinking, not theirs.

Colin Buchanan 26 September 1973

1 See the footnote on page 4 overleaf.

1 A CUMULATIVE CASE

This booklet is making a case. What sort of a case is it making? The answer is that a process is involved which is something like an advocacy in court. The case for the 'defence' is well known—that infants should not be baptised because infants *cannot* be baptised. 'Baptism requires repentance and faith on the part of the recipient, infants cannot have repentance and faith, therefore whatever rites or forms are used in connection with infants these cannot rank as baptism, and, lest through a resemblance to baptism in their outward form they mislead those parents, and indeed the whole people of God, we ought not to pretend by word or action that we are in fact giving baptism to infants'. That is the defence's case, like a simple plea of innocence. It is developed in a quantity of books[1], and it has a straightforward appeal in its 30-second form set out above. To many of the 'jurors' the verdict is settled even before the 'prosecution' is heard. How important then that the pedobaptist case be fully and weightily made.

There is in fact no difficulty in making the case at length—the difficulty is being made to match the 30-second exposition of the Baptist case above in a quick verbal interchange. *There is no 30-second short statement of the pedobaptist case.* But that of itself does not pre-judge the result of the hearing—in many a court a deceptively simple plea of innocence by the

[1] One can cite from recent years a very substantial (if by no means exhaustive) list of Baptist (or nearly Baptist) works published in Britain. Good examples are: J. Warns *Baptism* (Paternoster 1957), A Gilmore (ed.) *Christian Baptism* (Lutterworth 1959), R. E. O. White *The Biblical Doctrine of Initiation* (Hodder 1960), G. R. Beasley-Murray *Baptism in the New Testament* (MacMillan 1962—paperback Paternoster 1972) and *Baptism To-Day and To-Morrow* (MacMillan 1966), K. Barth *Baptism as the Foundation of the Christian Life (Church Dogmatics* Vol. IV Part 4, T. & T. Clark 1969), J. K. Howard *New Testament Baptism* (Pickering & Inglis 1970), and, though its reference to the rite of baptism is indirect, J. D. G. Dunn *Baptism in the Spirit* (S.C.M. 1970). Smaller works include Barth *The Teaching of the Church concerning Baptism* (S.C.M. 1948), Watson *Baptism not for Infants* (published by T. E. Watson 1962), Child *A Conversation about Baptism* (S.C.M. 1963), Cryer *By What Rite?* (Mowbray 1969) and Carson *Farewell to Anglicanism* (Henry Walter 1969). These all (except the small Barth) come since Marcel's *The Biblical Doctrine of Infant Baptism* (James Clarke 1953) was published in English and thus, quite apart from the powerful Jewett 'Syllabus' *Infant Baptism and Confirmation* mentioned on page 3, there stands in English a great body of Baptist literature virtually uncriticised by pedobaptists. The only pedobaptist contributions have been Cullman's thrusts against Barth in the unsatisfactory *Baptism in the New Testament* (S.C.M. 1950) and the dry controversy over the history of what *happened* between Jeremias and Aland—see Jeremias *Infant Baptism in the First Four Centuries* (S.C.M. 1960), Aland *Did the Early Church Baptize Infants?* (S.C.M. 1963) and Jeremias *The Origins of Infant Baptism* (S.C.M. 1963). The latter controversy is dry not only because it tackles history rather than theology, but also because Aland confesses that even if infants were not baptised in the first centuries, yet they should be to-day. One can in 1989 add the books cited on page 2 above. One could add to the list Osborn *Forbid Them Not* (S.P.C.K.) 1972) and, just before this edition goes to press, Mark Dalby *Open Baptism* (S'P.C.K. 1989), but this sort of universalist defence of indiscriminate infant baptism is an embarrassment to those who wish to make a more cautious and careful pedobaptist case. The best pedobaptist book of recent yevrs is Murray *Christian Baptism* (Presbyterian and Reformed U.S.A. 1970). There has of course been a series of writings on the relation of baptism to confirmation, but these are not concerned with the main issue here.

defence has to be met, and is successfully met, by a far more detailed and complex case for the prosecution.

The important point to be made here is that a 'case' is a case—it has to be marshalled in a cumulative way. All trials function on this 'cumulative' principle—and it is this which constitutes 'proof'. It is in fact *inductive* 'proof'. There is no other sort of proof possible in court, but it must be recognised that this form of 'proving' can still leave doubts, leave some persons unconvinced (so that a charge may now be 'proved' by a majority verdict of 10—2 on a jury), and may enable the other side thus honourably to protest the justice of its cause even when the verdict has been given. The doubts are particularly prone to arise when there are no eye-witnesses of the event being tried. The evidence is then circumstantial and has to be cumulated all the more carefully. Such is the sort of 'proof' with which we deal in the question of infant baptism. But because the case *is* circumstantial and cumulative, there is a sense in which the jurors have got to 'see' how the case fits—and if they do not, they do not. But it is also true that such cases *can* be virtually watertight and offer genuine proof.

Perhaps the point about a cumulative case can be made best with an imaginary instance. A man is known to be at odds with his wife, and to be spending time with another woman. One day he walks with his wife onto a high suspension foot-bridge in a fog. There is a cry, and she has fallen over and is dead. Unfortunately, there are no independent witnesses, and the evidence as to the truth will have to be circumstantial. But it is known that the man inherits a large sum of money in her will, and it can be shown that he knew not only that she was leaving him this money, but also that she had indicated to him her intention of changing the will and leaving her money to a cats' home. Furthermore he was financially embarrassed at the time of his wife's death. All these circumstantial facts are agreed between prosecution and defence. They are the basic data in the case. It is the interpretation to be placed upon them which differs.

The prosecution says that everything hangs together—means, motive, opportunity. In effect they say the case is overwhelming. Could any man entertain any reasonable doubt but that the man pushed his wife off the bridge in order that he might inherit the money, marry the other woman, and live happily thereafter? The agreed facts themselves, say the prosecution, immediately and irrefutably 'prove' the man's guilt.

Not so fast, comes back the defence. And the case for the man might be made by a series of 'special pleadings'. The defence says that *if* all the agreed facts belong closely with each other, then the man is indeed probably guilty. But they do not agree that the facts hang together—they are disparate data pushed together to make the case. It is true the man had another woman—thousands do, so what? That does not make every man whose wife dies into a murderer. It is true that he knew he would inherit if she died now, but would not if she lived to change her will. So what? Thousands of men have been in such a position without committing murder—and many of them have actually had their wives die soon after they came to such knowledge, without thereby committing murder. It is true that they went onto the suspension bridge together, and she fell off and he came back alone. But none of that makes him a murderer. And the defence can weave together other possible solutions to the same data—e.g. that they went together onto the bridge only because in fact they had just been reconciled (!), for had things been as the prosecution described them she would never have gone near the bridge with him. And there on the bridge the man was on one side looking over when he heard a scream and his wife fell over the other. An accident? Suicide? Murder by someone else who was there in the fog on the bridge unseen by the husband? Who knows? But the cumulative case, so the defence alleges, exists through putting together events which were actually coincidences. The more the coincidences stretch the credulity of the jurors, the better the cumulative case is doing, and the more obviously the defence is indulging in special pleading. But if the events grouped strike the jury as genuine coincidences (though somewhat surprising or even unique) then the defence will win.

So now in this particular debate between two positions on infant baptism. It is agreed on all sides that there are no independent witnesses, no straightforward apostolic accounts of the baptism of infants. We are then in a situation where the evidence must be circumstantial. The case *for* the propriety of infant baptism must therefore be a cumulative one—like the prosecution's in the murder case above. The Baptist 'defence' is in the first instance the simple plea of innocence—i.e. the sort of 30-second statement with which this chapter opens. In the second instance it will be a response of 'special pleading' to the cumulative case. As we go on to make the cumulative case it will be obvious that various processes and results are possible, and are possible without the honour or integrity of either side in the debate being brought into question. Firstly, the more relevant evidence which can be assembled, the stronger the case (and therefore in principle one would not expect a 30-second prosecution case where circumstantial evidence is needed). Secondly, the refutation of any one piece of evidence, or the showing that it is not, or might not be, relevant, may weaken the case without overthrowing it. Thirdly, the case might fall short of carrying total conviction and yet leave a suspicion that it was basically preferable, but needed a little more evidence to clinch it. Or it might carry conviction, yet leave a worried suspicion that a determined special pleading could win a technical verdict against it. Fourthly, the case might have to be put and then the advocacy should rest whilst the other side has a go. In such a situation the case might well establish a *prima facie* credibility (and thus remove it from the 30-second Baptist case), but the hearing would still continue and the other side would have to be heard. If this debate on an old issue brings new evidence in as relevant (and it *might*) then this need for the debate to continue would be strong. And in such a situation then the case here made might have to be re-adjusted and restated if a telling response is brought against it.[1]

In brief, whilst we conceded that those who repent and believe should be baptised, we do not concede that the statement can be reversed and smoothly applied to exclude all infants and children from baptism. All sheep may be animals without all animals being thereby sheep. Adult believers may well be true candidates for baptism, but it does not follow that the only true candidates for baptism are adult believers. There is a case for the baptism of the children of believers. That is the case put forward here.

[1] Prophetic words? In a sense this is exactly the rationale of Booklet no. 24.

2 SOME GENERAL POINTS ON BAPTISM

In brief compass like this, some theological points about baptism have to be asserted rather than demonstrated at length. The relevant ones follow.

Baptism is one and common to all Christians. This is surely the implication of Eph. 4.4—'one Lord, one faith, one baptism'. There can be no more a denominational baptism than a denominational Christ (which is exactly the thrust of 1 Cor. 1 also). Baptism cannot be simply a subjective experience—it must demand recognition by the Church through the world.

Baptism is once and for all and for life. Because it initiates (into the church, into salvation, into Christ, into the new life) it cannot be repeated. A person is either baptised or unbaptised. Once baptised he cannot become unbaptised again.

It follows that there must be a good rule-of-thumb definition as to what is to rank as a baptism. This is not pursued here, but is fully discussed in booklet no. 61, *One Baptism Once*.

It also follows, and this is in fact how it appears in the New Testament, that baptism must *prima facie* be treated as efficacious, as actually effecting what it signifies. Thus in the New Testament there is strong instrumental (or categorical) language about baptism—'Be baptised . . . and you will receive the gift of the Spirit' (Acts 2.38), 'Be baptised, and wash away your sins' (Acts 22.16), 'We were buried therefore with him by baptism into death' (Rom. 6.3), 'For by one Spirit we were all baptised into one body' (1 Cor. 12.13), 'As many of you as have been baptised into Christ have put on Christ' (Gal. 3.27), 'Baptism . . . now saves you' (1 Pet. 3.21)[1], and several others. None of these texts have to imply that baptism is always unconditionally efficacious without regard to other conditions, nor do they imply that somehow there is grace within the waters or originating from the baptism itself and not from God. But they do imply a strong case for understanding baptism in the New Testament as ordinarily effecting what it signifies.[2]

Because of the above factors, it follows that the baptised have a *prima facie* claim to be treated as Christians, and, to be treated as Christians by the Church, believers have a *prima facie* duty to receive baptism. No wedge should be driven between becoming a believer and receiving the sacrament.

This in turn means that we cannot be driven to either of the opposite poles of doctrine—one of which would seem to say that we baptise when we

---

[1] Of course some will object that these texts do not all refer to water-baptism at all (as, for instance, J. D. G. Dunn in *Baptism in the Holy Spirit* (S.C.M. 1970)). But this is a case of circular argument. It starts by affirming on other grounds that baptism in water cannot effect anything, then has to continue by insisting that texts which suggest that water-baptism *is* efficacious simply cannot be referring to water-baptism at all. This is not only a very dubious principle—it is also almost impossible to operate, as the texts from Acts, at least, are acknowledged on all sides to refer to water-baptism.

[2] For further discussion of this, see Booklet no. 61, *One Baptism Once*.

7

are persuaded that people belong to Christ, but not until then (which seems to mean that they are already initiated), and the other of which would seem to say that we baptise and thereby invariably *make* the recipients belong to Christ. If we have to choose—well it is arguable that the second position is nearer to the New Testament than the first. But we do not choose—we steer between. We baptise upon conditions, and affirm the efficacy of baptism upon those conditions. And we look for certain warrants prior to baptising which will suffice as presumptions upon which we can baptise—and then we treat baptism as truly initiatory.

If we adminster baptism on the basis of a rule-of-thumb warrant as a qualification for admission to it, this will be rrue whether we adminster it to adults or to infants. Even with adults that warrant is *bound* to be arbitrary. One congregation's rule-of-thumb may allow baptism at the point of enquiry, another's at the point of profession, another's after some instruction, and yet another's after the candidate has satisfied the church that a thorough inner conversion has occurred and has been demonstrated in life. This arbitrariness may bear in different ways upon the perceived efficacy of the rite, but, although each different discipline may plead that it is scripturally sounder or pastorally more appropriate than the others, each baptism that is administered under any discipline is to be recognised *as* baptism by those following a different discipline. The same is true in the case of infants: the quest for the right 'warrant' for baptising infants does not mean that baptism administered on the basis of a wrong warrant is not baptism – nor that any particular administration of baptism, even if on the basis of the right warrant, must be efficacious. And part of the task of this 'Case' is to bring Baptists to recognise that, however unwelcome infant baptism may be to them, yet it *is* Christian baptism.

One final general point needs to be made about method. The New Testament has considerable gaps in the evidence. This has led to a series of arguments and counter-arguments about the significance of silence. On the one hand the New Testament never calls a Christian minister a 'priest'— and this silence (amid the quantity of other words which is used) does seem significant. On the other hand the New Testament never mentions that women were present at holy communion, but this silence seems of no significance at all, because 'anybody can see that this is what was done'. Where does the lack of any straight statement that infants were baptised on a particular occasion fit in? It could leave us saying that no amount of defence of infant baptism can measure up against this lack. Or it could leave us saying that on other grounds 'anybody can see that this is what was done'. The success of the cumulative case is measured by how far the jurors begin to feel 'anybody can see that this is what was done'.

3 THE ANTECEDENTS OF BAPTISM

Antecedents are of interest insofar as they show us how the New Testament fulfilled or reinterpreted the Old, and they are also of interest if they show how Jewish minds might have thought in the first century A.D.

Antecedent 1—Circumcision

It has been traditional for pedobaptists to argue from the practice of infant circumcision (as the outward mark and sign of the Old Covenant) to infant baptism (as the outward mark and sign of the New). This does indeed remain an important part of the cumulative case to be presented, though it is also true that the value of it has frequently been overestimated. There are several stages to the argument:

1. Circumcision is originally the 'sign of the covenant' (Gen. 17.11). It is received by Abraham as an adult but it is to be given to his sons thereafter in infancy, when eight days old (Gen. 17.12, 21.4). In the New Testament, Paul says that Abraham received the sign of circumcision as a seal of the righteousness which comes through faith (Rom. 4.11)[1]. This would mean that the righteousness of Christ, reckoned to those who believe, is signified in circumcision under the Old Covenant (as we are elsewhere told that the Old Covenant believers were saved through the atonement of Christ (Rom. 3.25, Heb. 9.15)). But this sign was appropriately given to infants apparently. If baptism proves to be the New Covenant equivalent, ought it not also by parity of reasoning to be given to infants?

2. Baptism itself has the same significance, and this appears in the same letter of Paul's. In Romans 6, Paul appeals to conceded points as a basis for his call to a life of holiness. The great point he has established is this very principle of the reckoning of Christ's righteousness to believers. No other doctrine could ever have given rise to the possible objection 'Shall we continue in sin that grace may abound?' (Rom. 6.1). The answer is that being justified it is unthinkable to cling to sin.

[1] The RSV translation is here misleading, when it says 'as a sign or seal'. The orginal is clearly 'the sign of circumcision *as a seal . . .*' (our italics), and 'sign' and 'seal' are not inter-changeable. The most obvious reading is that circumcision was always a 'sign', and was in Abraham's case also a 'seal' (because he had already come to faith and been justified and therefore confirmation or assurance of his position before God was all that the sign could mean to him). But it is not unfair to construct from this that circumcision was in principle always a sign of the righteousness which comes through faith—even if the faith had long been present, as in Abraham's case, or was not overtly present at all, as in Isaac's. The role of the 'sign' as a 'seal' might vary, but its meaning as a sign would surely be consistent. A personal opinion is that the pedobaptists have not helped their case by trying to make baptism in principle a 'seal', by universalising the particular argument of Paul about Abraham in Rom. 4. It is hard to understand a seal which precedes in time that which it is meant to be sealing—and thus pedobaptists have been led on to say that it is the *promise* of righteousness which is 'sealed' in infant baptism— the baptism is a visible way of stating to the baby on what terms God will assuredly receive him later. This is all very well but it is different from adult baptism, and obviously qualifies all infants for baptism. So we stick to the concept of a sign, and leave the seal for Abraham (to whom Cornelius would correspond in baptismal terms (Acts 10.44-48)). But see also booklet 24, pp. 8-9, 14 and 21-22.

And Paul gives the answer not by invoking justification directly, but by invoking the fact of baptism. But it is clear that the signification of baptism ('burial with Christ', 'union with Christ in his death', 'he who has died is justified [*sic* Rom. 6.7] from sin') is this very reckoning of righteousness, and we are left giving the same meaning to baptism as to circumcision.

3. We may tighten up this identification as follows: circumcision also was once-and-for-all-for-life (obviously); circumcision also admitted into the fellowship of God's people on earth; circumcision also (as baptism here in Romans 6) required a new life of holiness (compare the phrase 'uncircumcised at heart' (Jeremiah 9.26), and see also Dt. 10.16); circumcision, because it was initiatory in character, set the boundaries of God's people (the Philistines were the 'uncircumcised'). Are not all these also characteristics of baptism as it appears in the New Testament? And were not all these features of circumcision appropriate in their application to infants and children under the Old Covenant? And if they were, would they not still be appropriate if given to infants and children to-day by baptism?

4. Lesslie Newbigin, in his book *The Household of God* (SCM 1953), has denied this comparison. He urges that if this identification were in the apostles' minds, then they would never have dealt with the 'circumcision' party in Acts 15 or Galatians by saying that circumcision was done away in Christ, and now we are justified through faith. They would have far more appropriately said 'Circumcision is replaced by baptism, so you now need not the former but the latter'. One can feel some of the force of this, whilst still ranking it very subjective. The main objection is that Paul is not opposing a healthy, but outdated, sacramentalism, against which he can now set a healthy and up-to-date sacramentalism. He is opposing a distorted and unhealthy legalistic sacramentalism, against which he chooses to resort to an annihilation of the legalism involved (by setting out the true doctrine of justification), rather than by taking the narrower argument which would involve an appeal to baptism, (but with still a strong emphasis upon the liberating effect of the gospel). Of course, if the early chapters of Romans are directed at all against judaisers, then Romans 6 is in fact indicating the role of baptism in relation to justification. Similarly if Colossians 2.11-12 has the actual *rites* of both baptism and circumcision in view[1], then the identification is perfectly natural and easy to Paul. Granted the argument from the theological *meaning* of both rites, it is hard to go with Newbigin.

---

[1] It may be naive to assert that the rites are in view in both cases in these verses, because the references to circumcision in particular look highly metaphorical. On the other hand the natural way in which the two terms are unself-consciously juxtaposed by Paul does raise the question whether he was not thinking of the two together even if he then spins a sophisticated theological argument round the terms he used. But this is no more than a straw in the wind, and we put it into the cumulative case only for what it is worth.

5. The Baptist has traditionally argued the *discontinuity* of the two Covenants, which would therefore imply a discontinuity of the role of their initiatory signs. The case goes like this: membership of the people of God under the Old Covenant was conferred *automatically* by birth, and it was hardly surprising if infants were then automatically enrolled with circumcision. But membership of the people of God under the New Covenant is 'not of blood' (John 1.13), and belongs only to those who respond to him. Thus the initiatory sign cannot belong to infants in the way the Old Covenant sign did[1].

6. The trouble with the Baptist argument for discontinuity is its failure to trace circumcision back to its source. In the first two generations from Abraham to Jacob succession was *not* automatic simply through birth. Membership of the people of God is declared in Scripture, as far as those two generations are concerned, to be by naked election.[2] It is *not* that the children of nature were also, by the very fact of birth in the family, the children of the promise, and the heirs of Abraham. In Galatians 4 Paul makes a large argument hang upon the difference between Ishmael and Isaac in the economy and purposes of God. The difference between the two sons in each generation is perfectly clear. The sheer fact of birth to a family which had been specially called of God did not of itself confer *any* automatic membership of the elect people of God. The fathers in each case circumcised both sons, as infants in every case but Ishmael's, but the circumcision, although it carried a divine significance, did not attest any *automatic* inheritance. Thus the Baptist argument here starts from a wrong presupposition about circumcision—it is not a fleshly, earthly sign, of a fleshly, earthly people of God. It is from the beginning the sign of God's election, which is given to the offspring of God's people without distinguishing at the point of birth how they are to grow up in the purposes of God. And here, perhaps, is a very cogent model for an

[1] I have been involved in a set-piece theological bedate on this issue, at Tyndale House Cambridge, with David Pawson. He put forward a fascinating theory that there *is* a continuity, in that the sign is still to be given to the new-born children of believers but that, as so many matters which appear in physical form in the Old Covenant have an inner spiritual (and non-physical) counterpart in the antitypes of the New Covenant, so the 'children' of believers are not those born to them physically, but those 'begotten in the gospel' by them (compare 1 Cor. 4.15, Gal. 4.19, 1 Peter 5.13, etc.). This is a splendid attempt to conserve both the elements of continuity and discontinuity in a consistent way, and is at first sight very satisfying. It has two defects: one, that it starts from a wrong presupposition about the role of circumcision in the Old Covenant (see paragraph 6 which follows); two, that it sounds awfully like the ingenuity of a man who is determined to stick to his conclusions, even if he has to scrap his previous arguments and go round looking for new ones. However, we are all prone to this, and I may well be open to the same charge. See David Ransom's exposition of this in booklet 24, p.12 (and also my reply there, pp.23-24).

[2] In the first generation the message is 'The son of this slave woman shall not be heir with my son Isaac' (Gen. 20.10), 'I will establish my covenant with Isaac' (Gen. 17.21). In the second generation it is 'Two nations are in your womb . . . the elder shall serve the younger' (Gen. 25.23) and 'Jacob have I loved but Esau have I hated' (Mal. 1.2-3). Note the use of these very texts and concepts in the discussion on election in Rom. 9.6.13.

understanding of the role of infant baptism. The rite of circumcision, in these normative archetypal cases[1], was a spiritual sign, fulfilling a somewhat different role from that which the Baptist tends to affirm as his starting-point in the discussion.

It must be admitted that pedobaptists, whilst very keen to invoke the 'covenant principle', have not stated it well. If they fail to grapple with the significance of circumcision in these two generations, then they tend to give half their case away before they start. Jewett in particular impales them neatly on the horns of a dilemma, when they start the argument from the later automatic inheritance of a place in the nation which is a large part of the administration of circumcision to infants in the rest of Jewish history. He points out that we are saying *either* that the children of believers are automatically by birth inheritors of the kingdom, *or* that the children of believers have all 'a special status within the covenant' which is not saving but is a privilege[2]. On the one horn the facts of the matter impale us. On the other the baptism given is not a proper initiation, is not comparable to adult baptism, and only adds up to a way of saying that the children concerned are in a good place to receive the gospel. It looks as though Calvin is impaled on the former horn, and latter-day Anglican evangelicals on the latter. But the first two generations which practised circumcision encourage us to give baptism to our new-born children, not rashly insisting that beyond all doubt they are automatically believers and inheritors of the kingdom, but equally firmly pointing out that they are to be treated as such unless or until the evidence of their lives points in the opposite direction. They start with a strong presumption in their favour, and we treat them accordingly. Thus we avoid the horns, and we also discover the first clues about bringing up Christian children.

For the moment, we set out as the beginning of the cumulative case the evidence from circumcision. Its tendency is strongly towards the baptism of the children of Christians.[3]

---

[1] Normative, because most Old Covenant evidence relates to these two generations. Archetypal, because they came first.

[2] Such a concept would produce an outward 'Christendom' in which baptism would not really mark out Christians from the world at all.

[3] Is it profitable to speculate *why* God should have replaced the one sign by the other— especially as the one left a permanent mark of initiation upon the recipient (which is the background to Paul's appeal to *the fact of being a baptised person here and now*—as opposed to simply remembering what it felt like to undergo the rite once long ago—compare Rom. 6.3-7, 1 Cor. 1 etc. etc.), and the other did not? One might hesitatingly suggest that the fact that women could receive baptism as well and as easily as men has something to do with it—there is a gospel liberty for women which the Old Covenant did not bestow. There is also the development of proselyte baptism, which is the likely Jewish background to the New Covenant use of baptism. These two different lines of thought in fact converge on inspection. But in any case we are left merely to speculate idly, whilst accepting that this was how God *did* work. See also the discussion on page 14 below.

Antecedent 2—Proselyte Baptism

We remain ultimately unsure whether proselyte baptism was in fact in use at the time of our Lord, but the usual conclusion is (hesitatingly) that it was, and that it originated because in the Roman Empire women, who by definition could not be circumcised, wished to become Jews by being proselytised and needed some ceremony to mark their changed allegiance. The situation was new in that they were acting on their own, independently of their husbands, in a way which would have been unthinkable or impossible in the centuries before. Jeremias gives a large part of his first book on the subject (*Infant Baptism in the First Four Centuries* (SCM, 1960)) to a consideration of the implications of such a practice for Christian baptism. In brief he shows a similarity of language about the theology of initiation, and a close similarity in the actual ritual practice of baptism. He also traces out the practice of baptising children (for the males received baptism as well as circumcision, whilst the females received baptism only), and although again the evidence for this comes from well into the Christian era, it is reckoned as a likely accompaniment of proselyte baptism from the very start of the practice.

Proselyte baptism was only given to infants and children when they were admitted to Judaism with their parents (or with one parent). As the practice had not existed until a late date, it was obvious from the Old Testament writings, and from the received traditions, that those born within Judaism did not need baptism, but had a clear status from the time of birth. However, we have here the missionary significance of household baptism which would include the children at the point of their parents' initiation. Thus if Christian baptism had any roots in proselyte baptism, then the presupposition would be strong that Christian baptism was given to children with their parents, and they were thus included with them in the covenant people of God.[1]

Antecedent 3—Johannine Baptism

It is probable that the baptism of John erupted onto Judaism against this background of an understanding of a proselyte baptism, which by definition was never given to anyone born within Judaism. The scandal of John's baptism therefore was that the rite which signified the purification and cleansing of the 'unclean' Gentiles was now, as a judgment and as a renewal, to be applied to the Jews themselves. God was judging his own people, to prepare from them a new people from whom his gospel would go out to the world. Whilst, therefore, Johannine baptism has no particular history or theology attaching to it which helps decide the question about

---

1 What then of the significance of the non-baptism of those born *within* Judaism? We should note that this did not apply to circumcision, which was always given to infants on the eighth day, and the Christian practice may at this point depend more upon circumcision than upon proselyte baptism. If the non-baptism of those born within Judaism were pressed it would prove too much. It would set up a situation where children born to believers were so involved tribalistically in their parents' faith, that they needed no baptism at all, neither as infants nor as adults, but were reckoned as initiated from the start. Jeremias states (*Infant Baptism in the First Four Centuries* p.47) that he had once held this view, but at the time of writing was less sure. This was in any case an inferential case from 1 Cor. 7.14. There is not a word otherwise, to the best of my knowledge, anywhere in the writings of the church at any date to suggest that this practice was ever actually followed.

the baptism of infants, it is a crisis in the history of initiation which draws together the leading points of the other two antecedents and becomes the crucible through which they pass to be transformed into Christian baptism.

The relation to circumcision is, obviously, to challenge and to supersede it. Though Jews who received John's baptism would remain circumcised, it was in the baptism that they were initiated into Christ[1]. With the passage of time, when it became clear over the decades that circumcision was unnecessary to membership of the Church, so the being circumcised became almost irrelevant, and it was the baptism which marked the beginning of discipleship. Perhaps this too goes a little of the way further towards answering the question in footnote 3 on page 12 above. Circumcision *had* to be replaced in the economy of God in order that Jews could be initiated into Christ in the first generation. Without the new rite there would have been no turning-point for the Old Covenant people.

The relation of Johannine baptism to proselyte baptism is immediately to make those born in Judaism proper candidates for baptism for the first time ever. The question then opens up—as missionary proselyte baptism had been given to parents with their children, as now the 'mission' is to Judaism also (and indeed begins there), would not parents and children alike qualify for this baptism into the Messiah? And would not children born to believing parents now also qualify?[2]

We thus conclude from the known antecedents that it is far more probable that first generation Jews who received baptism would also take their children and babes in arms into baptism with them than that they would not. Each of the three antecedents adds weight to the cumulative case.

[1] This is to assume that Johannine baptism *was* 'baptism into Christ'. This, rather against current thinking, I would like to suggest, though, if it was not, the implications are not serious for the position here maintained. But the evidence suggests: (1) that John baptised with a clear forward look and expectation towards the coming of the Messiah; (2) that John baptised with a clear reference to the coming of the Spirit also; (3) that he called for repentance; (4) that the disciples did not baptise themselves first on the day of Pentecost, but reckoned themselves already baptised (perhaps by John, possibly by Jesus or his disciples during his earthly ministry (compare John 3.26; 4.1-2)); (5) that John apparently continued baptising when told that Jesus had started doing so (John 3.22-27)—or was thought by the early Church to have done so, which is equally significant—when he must otherwise have realised that his own baptisms were now redundant. Against this there exists the one case of the 'disciples' at Ephesus (Acts 19.1-6) who had been baptised 'into John's baptism'. It is at least arguable that this was a *deficient* Johannine baptism, which, coming after Pentecost, but not including proper teaching about the Messiah or the Spirit, had to rank as a non-baptism from a Christian standpoint. (It is interesting that Apollos (Acts 18.24-28) who also had only Johannine baptism was not, as far as we can see, given Christian baptism, and this, I suggest, was the more normal practice).

[2] This is meant as a set of *theological* questions. It is impossible to probe into the *historical* question as to whether John himself ever baptised children or infants. It is simply to try to think our way into how the first generation of Christians, with these antecedents before them, would most naturally have thought about infants and initiation: because, on all accounts, however they thought, the thoughts they had were so totally natural as to require no discussion or controversy that has come down to us. Their view did not have to be set up by arguments—they just had it, it was so natural. But what was it?

4 THEOLOGICAL EVIDENCE FROM THE NEW TESTAMENT

We continue the making of the case by looking deeper into certain matters in the New Testament from which relevant evidence emerges. The process is admittedly one of 'construction' of a case—that is conceded from the start. Any circumstantial case must involve this.

1 The Time of Baptism

The 'time' at issue here is not in the first instance the time of life. It is the time in relation to conversion. And the Acts, and the rest of the New Testament speak eloquently and unmistakeably with but one voice—converts were baptised at the point of professing or receiving conversion. We can multiply instances—at Pentecost 3,000 people were baptised (Acts 2.41) *on the same day that they believed;* in Samaria people were baptised before it was clear that they had not received the Spirit (Acts 8.12-17)—Simon included; the Ethiopian eunuch received baptism at the most only hours after he first met Philip (Acts 8.36-38); Paul possibly lingered three days, but more sensibly is not reckoned to have been converted till the darkness left him in Damascus (Acts 9.17-18—compare Acts 22.16), and he was then baptised immediately; Cornelius received the Spirit when the rules said he was not supposed to, so Peter metaphorically shrugged his shoulders and without any delay gave him the one thing missing, baptism (Acts 10.44-48); baptisms were administered with the gospel, as part of its administration[1], wherever the apostles went. Perhaps, to round up the picture, the Philippian jailer provides the best example of all (Acts 16.33-34), for he was a Gentile, with no Jewish background, but he was baptised between midnight, when he was first affected by Paul's message, and dawn the next day, which came after he had been baptised. The picture is the same everywhere. The New Testament Churches had no catechumenate, no probationary period, no course of instruction prior to admitting adults to baptism—they were admitted the moment they professed faith in Jesus as Lord.

1 The equivalent in modern day terms would be for Dr. Billy Graham, say, to hire not only the Wembley Stadium for his evangelistic rallies, *but also the Empire Pool.* Then when 'enquirers' came forward the first question on the counsellor's card would be 'Are you already baptised ?'. If the enquirer was, he would be treated as a lapsed Christian (however far gone from the truth). If he was not baptised, and wished to repent and believe, he would be taken straight through to the Pool, given a few minutes' further counselling (if all was straightforward) and would then receive Christ and be received into Christ *in baptism*—and would then rejoice with the Church at his new birth. This is of course not done, and it is not done not only because the sponsors of such rallies are disagreed about baptism amongst themselves—and many no doubt would reckon that those who had been baptised as infants were not in fact baptised at all, and ought therefore to be given baptism if such a practice were to be followed (which would be highly divisive). It is also, and more importantly, not done because all the sponsors are tacitly so *agreed* with each other that in any case baptism has so very little to do with preaching the gospel and securing conversions, that it can easily be left out of this sort of evangelism and not arise as a problem at all. Well, perhaps it can, but in the beginning it was not so, and the early Church picture ought to be held onto as an ideal and as the key to understanding baptism in many aspects, not least, for instance, in respect of the language of efficacy used about baptism in the New Testament and in our ideals of evangelism.

This pattern in the New Testament means that on the whole the Baptist constituency has itself not understood 'believers' baptism' aright. Baptism is not an opportunity for witness later given to the convert (if it had been that the Ethiopian eunuch ought to have gone back to Jerusalem to be baptised in the presence of the Church), nor is it a point of personal obedience to which the Christian is brought as he studies the New Testament and thinks through the rite for himself, nor is it the reward the Church gives a convert when, after a period of testing, it concludes that the earlier profession of conversion was indeed genuine and the crowning recognition of this can be afforded to the person. No, baptism is *how the Lord and the Church make the man a convert*—make him a Christian, or a saint (which is more like the New Testament terminology)—or, in other words, it is how the Church grows and extends its frontiers. The New Testament knows nothing of an unbaptised Christian—the nearest approach is Cornelius, and the first thing to be done is to baptise him. In the congregations to which the New Testament letters are addressed it is axiomatic that all have been baptised, so that where he chooses (e.g. in Galatians 3.26-27) Paul can interchange an appeal to baptism (as applying to all the recipients) for the appeal to faith, which we would more naturally have expected from the arguments of the passage. One further point to note is that no catechumenate meant no certainty about the actual state of heart of many who received baptism. The hypocrite might well get baptised if he was to be put into the water without weeks or months of testing. He would still *be* a hypocrite, and the New Testament suggests that the Churches of the time had their share of these. But their very existence in the congregations is evidence that baptism was administered *at the very point of professing conversion.*

This pattern is laboured somewhat, because it is very arguable that the controversies of the present day are partly inspired through the fact that Baptists frequently do not understand or use aright 'believers' ' baptism. It is thus hardly surprising that they cannot follow the biblical argument to infant baptism, for they are not at the right starting-point.

The bearing of all this on infant baptism should be obvious. The question is 'At what age is the child of a Christian home *first* entitled to be treated as a Christian?'. Whatever the answer to that question may be, it is at *that* age that he or she must be baptised. Any delay beyond that first point involves a subtle change in the role of baptism. It ceases to be an initiation and becomes a witness or a reward. And it does not have those roles in the New Testament. We shall return to this point in chapter 7 below.

2 The place of children in the body

A large amount of the discussion of baptism above has been somewhat individualistic, and has related to actual benefits conferred on individuals in baptism. But at the core of New Testament teaching on the subject, there is a strongly corporate element which is too easily overlooked in debate. The New Covenant Church is a company of the redeemed, the bride of Christ, the temple of the Lord through the Spirit, and the body of Christ—to cite some of the biblical imagery. These terms suggest an organic whole, and in these terms incorporation into the body of Christ, for instance, is something akin to an organ transplant. A member of one body (for these purposes, of Adam) is cut from its living context and is grafted into the other. At the point of transfer the organ stands individualistically on its own, but the transfer plants it into a new context of living tissue, and increases that body by its arrival.

Now when we look again at the hypocrite, however defective his own personal standing before God, his relation to the people of God is clear— he has been incorporated, and is reckoned with them from his baptism, and is only excommunicated if his hypocrisy turns into some openly provable evil-living or unbelief. He belongs. He is 'one of us'. We do not even know which of our Christian friends he is. There may be no such hypocrite among the Christians we know. We treat them all *as* Christians.

If this is the status in the Church not only of the 'true believer' but even also of the hypocrite, what is the status of the children of believers? Are they one with us in the body of Christ? Or are they outside of Christ, awaiting admission and initiation when they either come to visible belief, or prove themselves in some stated or rule-of-thumb way?

The New Testament throws little light on this point, but perhaps what gleams it does throw provide helpful if scanty evidence. We attach little weight to 'suffer the little children'[1]. This sort of text surely says nothing about admission into the Church, which baptism involves, and can only be referred to baptism by making the latter very individualistic? It more probably refers (by acted parable) to the necessity for those who come to Christ (at whatever age) to come in child-like faith and simplicity.[2] But we do attach weight to the place young children occupied in the first century Church. Frequent injunctions are given them (e.g. in Eph. 6.1-3, Col. 3.20, 1 John 2.12-14), and they are treated as under obedience to the

[1] And doubly not since the publication of the book *Forbid Them Not* by R. R. Osborn (S.P.C.K. 1972) which makes a case for indiscriminate infant baptism (at least in England) with reliance on this text, as its title shows. Cullman too, with his doctrines of 'General Baptism' and 'Not forbidding', seems to run to universalism from this verse. If any think it *does* add weight, well and good. But it is a frail and unhelpful passage to put into the case offered to the unconvinced. The Mark Dalby book, *Open Baptism*, mentioned in the footnote on page 4, pulls in the same direction.

[2] The very mention of 'child-like faith' shows how shaky this text is as a justification for *infant* baptism. Comically enough in the history of liturgy the text was first used to justify a laying on of hands on candidates during their catechumenate. Then when the catechumenate was swallowed up in the baptismal rite itself (for it could have no separate existence in the Middle Ages when infants were the only candidates for baptism) the gospel reading in the Sarum use became Mt. 19.13-15, though it was still clearly in the preliminary 'church-door' part of the rite. Cranmer then altered this to Mk. 10.13-16 in 1549, and integrated the 'church-door' part of the service with the rest in 1552. In both his rites there appears a justification for infant baptism resting upon this Markan account. We have seen that the case cannot be made in ten seconds anyway (and therefore no attempt to make it should be done in prayers or exhortations within the rite), but how totally impossible it is to make it in ten seconds *from this text!* It is not surprising that pedobaptists have often found their own case embarrassing—with such help from our friends, what need have we of antagonists?

law (in the normal Christian sense of those words) in Eph. 6.1-3. It is implicit throughout that their Lord is our Lord, they *are* one with us in him. And whilst this may not go so far as to suggest *infant* baptism, it does, in the light of our other baptismal principles, suggest that *children* at least received baptism, a position which inevitably starts to drive us in an asymptotic path towards the baptism of infants.

3. The 'holiness' of children

1 Cor. 7.14 refers to a point conceded on both sides of the discussion in which Paul is involved, that the children of believers, or of one believer, are 'holy' (or indeed are 'saints'—the word used in the New Testament of Christians). Here is a word which is opposed to 'unclean', and the opposition of these two words takes us immediately into the realm of Old Covenant ideas about the status of Jews (holy) and of Gentiles (unclean). The status is apparently conferred on the offspring of a believer *merely by being the offspring,* without reference to any further qualifications or qualities in himself. Whatever it means, it includes infants as easily and naturally as children of any other age. And, on what we have seen so far, then if the children were 'holy' they obviously ought to have been baptised, and presumably (though this is not explicit, maddeningly, as it is not the point of Paul's argument) were.

Once again an argument can be deceptive by being too simple, and before the pedobaptist treats his case as unanswerable, we ought to note that whatever 'holiness' the children have, that same 'holiness' is enjoyed by the *unbelieving adult partner* (1 Cor. 7.13-14). The same argument is involved—the 'holiness' is either conveyed to the partner in the same way that it is conveyed to the child, *or* it is conveyed to the child because, by this relationship between the partners which ensures that there are two 'holy' parents, the child receives the status from the shared 'holiness' of the parent. Any argument which leads to the propriety and desirability of baptising the child should also lead to the propriety and desirability of baptising the unbelieving partner also. And the Christian conscience does not like this conclusion.

On the other hand, even the Baptist must make *something* of this passage. The alternative interpretation usually favoured is that 'sanctifies' means 'legitimises' (i.e. although an unbelieving partner according to Paul may depart, the believer has no right without this action from his or her partner to assume that the other's unbelief has already sundered the marriage-bond, rather his or her own status is so conveyed to the other as to undergird the propriety of the marriage)—and the children are, as the basis of the argument, 'holy', i.e. 'legitimate'. This makes good sense in context, enabling a consistency between the application of 'holiness' words to partner and to children to be maintained. But is it the proper meaning of 'sanctify' and 'holiness'? Only in the previous chapter Paul seems to make 'sanctifying' a fruit of baptism (1 Cor. 6.11), and it is an odd wrenching of the meaning which seems to be involved on this 'legitimising' interpretation.

Of course, the two views are very near each other in what they are saying in context. On the 'holiness' view, Paul, is saying that if there are no *grounds* for divorce, because in some real deep sense it is not a 'mixed marriage' at all. On the 'legitimacy' view, Paul is saying there is no *fact* of divorce, as that which might have sundered the marriage is overridden by another principle. It is possible virtually to assimilate the two views in commentating, and the very fair commentators tend to do so. Thus C. K. Barrett[1] is on the one hand ready to say that the 'holiness' words 'must therefore be used in this verse in a sense differing from that which is customary in Paul.' But, on the other hand, a few lines later he says 'The children are within the covenant; this could not be so if the marriage itself were unclean.' Whilst he is unwilling to make any case for infant baptism from these verses, he does here produce a point of departure ('within the covenant') for such a case, but equally he is not willing to allow in so many words that the unbelieving partner is 'within the covenant'.

We conclude that this verse is of marginal relevance, but it may add some little weight to the cumulative case for infant baptism, and might well have been a more natural thing for Paul to say if he were used to baptising infants and children, than if he were not.

4 The withholding of communion from infants and children

Part of the theological argument of the Baptist has been an accusation to the pedobaptist of a bad conscience, betraying his lack of conviction about his own practice (with the inbuilt further suggestion that he clings to pedobaptism for unworthy reasons). The accusation comes in the form 'Every argument for infant and child baptism is equally an argument for infant and child communion, but you do not prvctise the latter so it is difficult to believe you mean business with the former—in fact we suspect that you baptise infants because you inherited the practice (though you go on thinking up reasons for it), and you reject infant communion because you did *not* inherit it (though when pressed you will think up reasons for your practice here too).' Historically, in this writer's opinion, the Baptist has had the better of this argument. The pedobaptist has gone on thinking up reasons for not giving infants and children communion, but they have looked like evasions to the accuser. The necessity of holding both sacraments together in our practice is very strong, and the New Testament is as silent on non-communicating baptised persons as it is on non-baptised believing persons.

Here we need not concern ourselves with these traditional replies to the charge. For the time has come to admit the force of the objection. This we can cheerfully do, and then advocate infant and child communion, as the comcomitant of infant and child baptism. The two *do* go together, and it is about time we acted accordingly.[2] This reply cuts the ground from under the Baptist controversialist[3], and he has to take up other ground.

All these points coinhere to tighten and strengthen the case for infant baptism.

[1] In *The First Epistle to the Corinthians* (Black 1968) on 1 Cor. 7.12-14.

[2] A thorough case for this can be found in Liturgical Study no. 44, *Nurturing Children in Communion*. But I cannot pretend that this form of reply to the Baptist accusation will appeal to all pedobaptists, and there will be many to defend a later age for 'admission to communion'. They make the argument more difficult for themselves. It is sad that, sixteen years on from when I first wrote, the Church of England has still not taken this step.

[3] Thus Jewett, for instance, gives 5,000 words to refuting pedobaptist defences of delaying the age of admission to communion.

5 HISTORICAL EVIDENCE FROM THE NEW TESTAMENT

We come now to the passing bits of evidence that not only was it right and appropriate to baptise infants and children in the New Testament times, but the Christians then thought so too, and did practise pedobaptism.

1 The Baptism of Households

In three places in the New Testament there is specific reference to the baptism of households: that of Lydia (Acts 16.15), that of the Philippian jailer (Acts 16.33), and that of Stephanas (1 Cor. 1.16). It is also possible that household baptisms were involved in the cases of Cornelius (Acts 10.48 compare 11.14) and of Crispus (Acts 18.8, but note 1 Cor. 1.14 where the household is not mentioned); these however have problems and the three first-mentioned households will suffice. The occurrence of household baptisms is exactly what we would have expected from our survey of both the antecedents of Christian baptism and the New Testament theological matters. And, sure enough, here they are—we ought to feel like the astronomers who discovered Neptune first of all by plotting it from the statistics of its 'pull' on Uranus, and secondly by turning their telescope to the part of the sky the calculations indicated. The two fitted—the object they found could not but be the new planet. So with us—the case is strong even before we look for the actual phenomenon, it is vastly increased when we find it where we would calculate it should be.

But there is one snag. Although we know 'households' were baptised, there is no specific mention of infants. Jeremias takes this one head-on. 'This [the concept of a household] does not mean to say that in every particular case in which the baptism of "a whole household" is mentioned, small children were actually present. But it does mean that Paul and Luke could under no circumstances have applied the *oikos* formula, if they wished to say that only adults had been baptized.'[1]

The Baptist reply to the phenomenon of household baptisms is, as might be expected, to try to deal with them one by one to show there were no infants involved. Thus, for instance, Lydia was the head of her household, so she had no husband, and therefore had no young children[2]. Stephanas' house is noted for its leadership (1 Cor. 16.15), which would be inconceivable from young children.[3] Cornelius' house boiled down to those 'who heard the word' (Acts 10.44), which obviously excluded babes in arms[4].

---

1 *Infant Baptism in the First Four Centuries* pp.21-22.
2 But this will not do. By all accounts she *did have a household.* So either she had children (and why not young ones if she were recently widowed?) or her household was composed of slaves, in which case again there was no reason why there should not be young children or infants involved.
3 This objection may be simply ignored. It is possible in England to-day to say that a certain family is a leading family in the town, without necessarily implying it has no young children (who could not be exercising leadership in it). A family can be said to have characteristics which are inappropriate to young children, without excluding the existence of young children. Obvious uses to-day are to say that a family is very tall, very talkative, very brave or cowardly, and so on. Any of these descriptions is possible even of a family including babies.
4 The Cornelius' point may or may not be acceptable. We do not need to make anything of Cornelius in the first place.

Crispus was baptised on his own, *without his household* (1 Cor. 1.14)[1]. The jailer does not have a 'household' with the *oikos* word at all—he merely rejoices 'wholehouseholdwise' (a single Greek adverb) when he personally is baptised and believes.[2]

We suggest that the initial case stands unless it is knocked about a lot more. Households, including persons of *all* ages, were baptised in New Testament times. It is a counsel of despair to dismember them. Even Aland concedes 'The "house" is saved when the head of the house is saved'[3].

It is still true that infants are not explicitly mentioned in these baptisms. If they had been, no problems would have arisen. The argument here is that the admissibility of infants is thoroughly in accord with these texts, and the prohibition of them is not. The 'households' are strong evidence, embarrassing to the Baptist.

2 Children in Church

We have noted above that our children are properly one with us in the body of Christ. We turn now to the evidence of New Testament history, and piece together further information about the children. We know that they were present in the congregation when letters from Paul were read out. We know they were probably exhorted to obey their parents 'in the Lord' (Eph. 6.1)[4]. We find in Colossians not only that they were specifically addressed by Paul (Col. 3.20), but also that in the chapter before the recipients were reminded that they had been baptised (Col. 2.12). This, we suggest, is the standard pattern. Children were there in the congregation from very early infancy, and were addressed as baptised persons there, because they had in fact been baptised straight after birth.

3 The Day of Pentecost

'The promise is to you and to your children'—said Peter on the Day of Pentecost (Acts 2.39). Then the 3,000 were baptised. Were there children baptised with their parents then?

The text itself is not immediately conclusive, but it leans quite heavily towards child, and perhaps infant, baptism. The hearers of Peter were there from all over the Mediterranean. In many cases they would have had their children with them. They included *proselytes* (Acts 2.11), a class only mentioned four times in the New Testament. And the proselytes would have already been baptised and circumcised into Judaism, *with their children.* They were now invited to be baptised into Christ (Acts 2.38). They were told the promise (which meant the Holy Spirit, Acts 2.33) was for them, *and their children* (Acts 2.39). How could they *not* now take their children with them into baptism?

1 Crispus must (unusually) have been separated from his household for the purpose of baptism, and Paul is of course reporting something unusual here. Were 'all his house' (1 Cor. 18.8) below some age-limit (including his wife if he had one)? If so, this could have serious implications for the meaning of *oikos* elsewhere! If not, then on any account Crispus was separated from the rest of his household at the time of baptism, and both sides are equally in the dark as to why.

2 This 'wholehouseholdwise' adverb does include the notion of a household. Was he too in Crispus' case? Or why does this not mean that he believed (with his household —according to their years) and was baptised (with his household) and rejoiced (with his household—according to their years)?

3 *Did the Early Church baptize Infants?* (S.C.M. 1963) p.91.

4 'Probably', because there is some manuscript doubt about 'in the Lord' (RSV).

6 AFTER THE APOSTLES

The Baptist case is neatly assisted by the fact that no undisputed historical evidence can be found for the existence of infant baptism after the time of the apostles until Tertullian's writings, around 200. Then at last, in the *De Baptismo,* the evidence arises—only to take the form of a protest against the practice. Why was there a silence? Because there was no infant baptism. Why was there then a protest? Because it was being improperly introduced? Why was there a great string of evidence thereafter? Because the pedobaptists won, and established their innovation as the Church's custom? The picture adds up very nicely.

But there is an alternative case, and it is probably more cogent. In the first place, there are only very scattered references to baptism at all in the period 100-200 A.D., and most of these could include children and infants, although such categories are not mentioned. In the second place, there must have been some *tradition* of infant baptism before 200. In the West, Hippolytus (around 215) records the baptism of those unable to answer for themselves, and does so in a document labelled *The Apostolic Tradition.* This purports to contain the received traditions from the apostles, and for its own purposes could not easily contain items which any contemporary knew had only arisen in the last decade or so.[1] Similarly in the East, Origen says 'The Church received from the apostles the tradition of baptising infants too'[2]. This was written after 240 it seems, but Origen's year of birth is normally reckoned at 185, he says himself that he came of a Christian family, and if he could even think that infant baptism was an apostolic practice, he must surely have been baptised as an infant himself. Otherwise, he would know from his own experience that the practice was an innovation in his own lifetime. If this is so, we can push the question back further—from where did Origen's parents get the idea that their child should be baptised? Tradition does have some value, and may we not here be stumbling upon an authentic apostolic tradition?

What then of Tertullian? No-one can decide absolutely whether it was infant baptism which was the innovation, or the protest against it which was. But there is one straw in the wind which we can catch. Tertullian does *not* use the favourite authority of his times (which we have seen just above). He does not say, as it would be conclusive if he could say, that infant baptism does not come from the apostles. This straw suggests that he had always known the practice, and so argues somewhat rationalistically, and not from tradition, against it. (Of course he should just have pointed out that it is not there in the Bible, but that too no-one of his time had stumbled upon!). Why then the new protest against infant baptism? Here too we can only speculate. Jeremias says that it was solely against the baptism of children from pagan homes, but we need not go that far

---

[1] It is significant that Aland (in his reply to Jeremias' first work on the subject *Infant Baptism in the First Four Centuries*) obviously would like to feel that this reference in Hippolytus is an interpolation of a later date, as in its present context the passage in Hippolytus is very damaging to Aland's case (see *Did the early Church baptize Infants?* (SCM 1963) p.49, referring to *The Apostolic Tradition* xxi.4).

[2] *Commentary on Romans* (re 6.5-7).

(Aland may be on better ground here). There only has to be a shift in rationale for infant baptism, and the protest is necessitated in a way it had not been before. Tertullian objects that sponsors are brought into danger by the waywardness of their godchildren as they grow up, and it would be better for the children to make their own decisions on maturity. But this reflects the growing concern for a 'pure' church which led to long catechumenates for adults[1] and inevitably brought infant baptism into question. The growth of this concern can be traced through the second century, and, even if we had not got Tertullian's text, we might almost have expected a protest against infant baptism to arise in the wake of this tendency.

In any case the argument which propounds an exhaustive moral answerability of the sponsor, even to the point of being under the judgment of God because of the way of life of the growing godchild, looks like an innovation. It is entirely consistent and sensible therefore to see Tertullian's protest as directed against a novel – and unacceptable – *basis* for baptising infants, rather than against a novel *practice* of baptising them.

We conclude therefore that Tertullian is on balance more of a witness for the probability of infant baptism being a received tradition in his times, than the opposite. And if we think this at all likely, we can throw in for good measure the other tiny hints which Jeremias gathers from that period.

These hints are as follows:

1. Polycarp at his martyrdom is said to have declared 'Eighty-six years I have served him [Christ], and he never did me any wrong . . .' This can be dated at around 155-168, and takes Polycarp's life or discipleship back to around 70-82. It is almost unthinkable that he was in fact 100 and had been a disciple since the age of 14 (for he travelled from Smyrna to Rome to meet Anicetus some time after 150, and if he had been nearing 100, or even 90, then that would surely have been a subject for special comment in either the account of the visit, or even more likely of the martyrdom. There were very few centenarians in those days anyway. So, when Polycarp said he had served Christ for eighty-six years, did he mean that he had served him as a child, but only been baptised later, or did he mean that he had been baptised as an infant eighty-six years before, and served him faithfully since? Or *must* his discipleship be dated back to a point no earlier than, say, fourteen years of age?

2. Justin in his *First Apology* (around 150) speaks of 'many men and women of the age of sixty and seventy years who have been disciples of Christ from childhood' (15.6). In point of fact the word translated 'have been disciples' is in the passive (i.e. 'were made disciples') and is used in this way elsewhere in Justin to refer to baptism. Had these elderly Christians in Rome been baptised in infancy (the words 'from

---

1 Thus Aland has to posit a long catechumenate in the *Didache* (around 115 A.D.), although the text only refers to two days' fast before baptism. The two points always go together—a catechumenate or probationary period before adult baptism entails a reaction against infant baptism, and the apostolic way of doing adult baptism happily accepts infant baptism. The argument against a catechumenate for adults as the New Testament practice is described on pages 15-16 above.

childhood' could include infancy) around 80-100? Aland says the actual description of baptism in *First Apology* 65-7 excludes any possibility of Justin knowing about infant baptism. This does not follow—Hippolytus describes what adults *did,* but he also tells us infants were present. So Justin's description of adult procedures would not preclude the presence of infants if as and when necessary. Significantly Aland does not then comment on the Justin passage mentioned above suggesting infant baptism in Rome *sixty or seventy years* earlier. Even if he were right about practice in Justin's day— and it is difficult to believe he is right—he still cannot solve so simply the question about the Christians who were elderly in Justin's day.

3. There are further hints of a similar sort in Aristides (writing around 130), Polycrates and Irenaeus (writing around 190). There may even be a hint in Pliny (writing in 112). In all these cases, if there are references to infant baptism, then the references take us into the first century, or the earliest part of the second.

For the moment, we do not rely upon any of these further hints as 'proving' an apostolic tradition. We merely affirm that *if* pedobaptism was in fact being practised from the apostles onwards, then there is at intervals evidence of its existence in the literature of the period—which affords confirmation of its existence. And if it was *not* being practised, then there are at intervals odd bits of evidence which need some explaining away. From the point of view of the overall cumulative case we note that the supposed silence on the subject from the apostles till Tertullian is not as total as is sometimes alleged, and the Baptist case gains nothing from these two centuries, if anything rather losing a little.

7. THE PROBLEMS OF THE BAPTIST

There frequently comes a turning point in a trial, when the defendant goes into the witness box and is cross-examined. The prosecution tests his story for chinks and inconsistencies, and the defendant under cross-examination may well clinch the case for the other side. We therefore turn now to see how the Baptist understanding and practice of baptism undergirds his stance against pedobaptism. There are four main searching questions we wish to address to him.

1. How will you bring up your own children?

If Christian parents are unwilling to have their child baptised in infancy, then obviously the child is unbaptised until such age as he or she does become a candidate for the sacrament. In New Testament terms to leave a person unbaptised is to declare that he or she is not a Christian. This is a viewpoint some Christian parents would apparently accept, and where they do, then they will seek to lead the child to know Christ later as he or she grows. This is all consistent and understandable.

However, it immediately creates consequential problems. In the first place, are such parents prepared to accept an expression of faith in Jesus at, say the age of two, as the evidence the child has now been converted? If they are not, then they are likely to postpone baptism to a point several years after the coming of conscious faith (for surely two-year-old professions may well be genuine?). And if they so postpone baptism, then when it comes it will have no relationship to the beginning of the Christian life, and will be a far departure from this particular New Testament principle, which we strongly aver. To continue during these years unwilling to accept the child's profession as genuine (when it really is) would also seem very damaging to the relationship in Christ which parents and child ought to have with each other. If the parents are to keep on asking themselves and the child whether he or she really understands what he or she is saying is to create unease where there ought to be confidence.

However, if the parents are willing to accept the proffesion as true they are still faced with the question of whether to baptise or not. If they *will* baptise, then they are steadily moving themselves towards pedobaptism again. Few people can think that the mere ability to say (perhaps with the child repeating parental phrases taught to him or her) 'I love Jesus' is *the* turning-point in a life. If this is to accepted (when any two-year-old can be coached into it) then surely the child might just as well be accepted *in toto* even before he or she says it, and the waiting for the first articulation is a wholly artificial concept. A pedobaptist need have no fear but that any parents who will bring a two-year-old to baptism are within a hairsbreadth of being pedobaptists themselves. The case is however a theoretical one – Baptist parents and Churches do not often impale themselves on *this* horn of the various dilemmas.

Will the parents then accept the profession as genuine, but delay baptism just the same? If they do, then they are forbidding the waters of baptism to those whom they deem the Lord to have accepted—exactly the situation Peter was concerned to avoid in Acts 10.44-48. And once again they will be in the anomalous position of treating as Christian one whom they are not prepared to mark as Christian with baptism. The child will be allowed to have a personal relationship with the Lord, but not in such a way that he or she can be incorporated by baptism into the fellowship of believers. (Or, if membership and incorporation are thought to come *without* baptism, then we are again driven to the place where baptism is solely a witness to events long past, or a Sunday School prize at the age of 11 or so, or an item in the personal path of discipleship which may come at any particular stage in the Christian life, or indeed at none[1].) Against this intricacy of inconsistencies we affirm again that to baptise is the natural and scriptural concomitant of treating someone as Christian.

Suppose again, that parents are determined *not* to accept the profession of faith of their two-year-old as genuine, or indeed not to encourage or even allow him or her to profess faith at all (as not being old enough to understand what such a profession could mean). Against this we make three counter-assertions. In the first place it is unscriptural for Christian parents to bring children up except 'in the Lord'. In the second place, it is psychologically damaging to exclude the child from the family circle in the way implicit in treating the child as an unbeliever. And in the third place, the programme is quite impossible to execute (fortunately), as even the most innocent attempt to get the child to pray or sing hymns must have an element of *inclusion*, of treating the child as trusting the same Saviour as the rest of the family. So we return again to the question—are Baptists content with a half-way inclusion, which leaves the child still uninitiated in New Testament terms?[2]

To all this a Baptist may reply—'Ah, but how can you *know* that such a child is *truly* believing if you give him baptism at birth, or even at two or three years of age?'. To this we direct attention again to the New Testament way of doing *adult* baptisms. If baptism is given within minutes of profession of conversion, how can we *know* that even *adults truly* believe when we baptise them? And the answer is, we cannot. Only the angels ever really *know* in that way. We on earth baptise on presumption, given certain warrants. The profession of repentance and faith is the warrant for an adult, the birth into a believing family is, we assert, the warrant for an infant. If we have to *know* a candidate's heart before we give baptism, then we shall never give it to anyone ... The wrong criterion for administering the sacrament is a poor basis for excluding infant baptism in believing families. We are going back to the 'catechumenate' error.

We may add yet one more point. People are what they are treated as being. Evangelicals have feared lest they confirm congregations in hypocrisy by

[1] One of the curious phenomena of Baptist principles in action is that many *adult* believers never get round to baptism, as in fact the sacrament is so personal and individual and a matter of taste (or at most of subjective conviction), that people make up their minds at their own speed. And once the Christian is well settled in Church life, then to ask for baptism can seem incongruous, and the more so as the years pass.

[2] It is this 'full inclusion' point which clinches the case for infant and child communion also—a case accepted on page 19 above.

telling them they are 'all right' because they have been baptised. But in fact the apostolic appeal for holiness of life is often based upon an appeal to baptism in this way. And if as and when we treat our children as regenerate from earliest days, this is exactly what we may expect in the goodness of God that they will prove to be. It is certainly *prima facie* the proper approach to bringing them up. But baptising them is part of treating them as regenerate and as children of God. Withholding baptism is to slant the sense of 'probation' (which the Bible does not countenance) too strongly. It is to ask the children to show signs of grace before you give them the means of grace.

2. When can a child believe?

If the point is conceded that believers should be baptised immediately they do believe, then we pursue our cross-examination by asking the Baptist to set up a minimum age for true belief, at least within the Christian family. Whilst we are well aware that some Christians can confidently assert that they were 'converted' at the ages of five, six, or seven, we wonder whether they were in a position to report this clearly at the time. Certainly where children have been treated as Christians, we would not expect there to be such a conscious crisis as the ability to report a conversion would presuppose[1]. And if they are not to be treated as Christians then the pressures upon them to profess faith, in terms they have been taught, must surely be such that parents are likely to be sceptical as to whether profession *does* imply true faith. As noted above, we deprecate this latter approach as unbiblical and unhelpful.

But the Baptist position more often seems to be that we are not justified in treating repentance and faith as genuine until much older years. So we press the question again—are young children not allowed by Church discipline to be true believers? Is this 'age of discretion' scriptural? What connection has baptism at this age with the beginning of the Christian life? What is the status in the Church of the unbaptised who are simply waiting for the years to pass till they can be accepted at the baptistry? And what is the status of a baptism which *is* given below the age of discretion? We suggest that the Baptist under cross-examination is distinctly uneasy when these questions are pressed. And this would hardly be surprising *if* his 'system' is man-made rather than based upon what we learn of baptism in the New Testament. *'If . . .'*

[1] To put this another way—it is not that one day a child comes face to face with the Saviour and makes a conscious decision. It is that, growing up in a home where the Saviour is known, only slowly does it dawn upon the child that there are odd people (at school and elsewhere) who are trying to live life on their own. One could go further into the psychology of this. Is it, for instance, probable that the parents stand *in loco Dei* from the earliest moments, and the transfer of devotion to God himself by the child is a gradual and unselfconscious process which he or she cannot possibly be expected to report accurately? If so, we are surely best trying to treat the child as a believer in the true God, rather than try to catch the child at the point of the watershed, and baptise him or her then. It is not, after all, that the child is passing from heresy to faith—it is that God himself has chosen to reveal himself to the child in this way, and the faith in a parent who is *in loco Dei* is to be accepted as faith in God. Consciousness, we say, *dawns*. But who can say when dawn begins? Many psychologists would say *this* dawn begins before birth.

3. What is the place of the unbaptised in the Church?

Assuming that Baptist ways of acting leave a gap between the point of belief and baptism, what is the Church to make of children (or indeed adults) in the meantime? As the only rite of membership is baptism, it is impossible in New Testament terms to make the person a member of the Church. It is impossible to affirm one Lord, one faith, one baptism in common with the unbaptised. It is impossible to appeal to the common ground of baptism to promote holiness of life (as, e.g., in Romans 6—which must fall on deaf ears to the unbaptised). It is impossible, if they wish to belong to Christ in any recognisable way at all, to do anything but baptise them.[1] And if the local Church has, by solemn advance forethought and Baptist convictions, vowed that it will *not* baptise children under, say, 11 years of age[2], or will *not* baptise adults until they have been through a period of probation, then there is no way, as far as the New Testament is concerned, in which they can 'belong' with Christ's people at all. Baptism *is* incorporation.

4. What is basic to the definition of a baptism?

Although Jewett goes a long way with the case for baptising adults on 'profession' of faith (recognising that no-one can know another's heart for certain), yet there is a strong suspicion that Baptists in the last analysis make the very validity of baptism depend upon the state of heart (and mind) of the recipient. Dunn in what he calls an 'epigrammatic' summary says that the New Testament teaches 'Baptism demands faith for its validity'[3].

It is obvious that such criteria mean that no 'infant baptism' is a baptism at all. The infant's heart and mind cannot be set on God at all. It is not surprising on these premises if Baptists treat those who have been baptised as infants as still needing baptism. But the premises deliver us to a horribly subjective understanding of the rite. We equally cannot know for certain whether the *adult* 'has faith' (and certainly not if we baptise the very time he or she professes conversion). We may enter the name on a baptismal register, only to discover later that faith was, on the person's own admission, lacking.

---

[1] There are of course Baptists who say that baptism must come when the Christian reaches a conviction about it, and asks for it. But this is to say that there will be no teaching about baptism in the Church, lest it load the decision of those who should be slowly finding their way to their own choice. It means that no-one should be urged to be baptised, and that baptism is viewed solely as an individual step in discipleship (as might be, say, a decision to remain celibate), and nothing of a churchly nature at all. It is surely both wrong and impossible to expect growing children, Christian or not, to find their way to scriptural convictions on the point without being under any pressure? And if they are under pressure, who can be sure it is their own decision?

[2] It is of course possible for Baptists to say there is no minimum age (except that infant baptism is not baptism!). But even where this is said, there must surely be a local consensus that the congregation would not expect a candidate to be brought to baptism below *some* age, though the actual age might vary from one place to another? Are there Baptist congregations which will baptise two- and three-year-olds on profession of faith?

[3] *Baptism in the Holy Spirit* (S.C.M. 1970) p.228. Note that Dunn does not say 'efficacy' (which would be understandable) but 'validity', which is perilous.

If faith is necessary for there to be a baptism at all, then ought not the name to be retrospectively erased from the roll? Two persons went through the waters of baptism on a particular date, but we later discover that one was baptised and one not! The latter may then be converted, and apparently qualify for a once-for-all baptism *de novo*. There is some reason to think that this has actually happened on occasion. It is certainly where the argument would take us. We therefore reaffirm against it that baptism is true Christian baptism where the administration of water is performed with some expression of its uniting to Christ or to the Trinity, in an orthodox Christian context. The faith of recipients is very important, but if it is lacking, that does not mean that there was no baptism. The baptism remains valid.[1] So it is with infants who are baptised.

---

[1] This is surely the point in 1 Corinthians 10? Paul says 'Our fathers . . . were all baptised . . . but with not all of them was God pleased, and they perished . . . and these things are written for our warning.' He could not write this unless on the one hand he accepted the *fact* of the baptism of 'all' the Corinthians, and on the other the lamentable (presumably 'unconverted') state of 'some' of them. But the subjective criteria for the validity of baptism would result in his saying 'All our fathers went through the Red Sea, but not all were baptised. All you have undergone an outward rite, but not all are baptised.' The New Testament says this sort of thing in a metaphorical way about circumcision (Romans 2), and does refer (rarely) to a 'baptism of the Spirit'. But it leaves actual water-baptisms inviolate in their status *as* baptisms, and appeals to the significance of the baptism to move the sluggish and uncommitted on in Christian discipleship. Here is a model for approaching those who have infant baptism, and not much else that is Christian. The question of the *definition* of a baptism is further pursued in Booklet no. 61, *One Baptism Once.*

8. LOOSE ENDS FOR PEDOBAPTISTS

All the above should take the case for infant baptism at least as far as being highly probable, or, I should like to think, fairly convincing. It does, however, leave certain loose ends, and a closing task is to tie up some of these.

1. Liturgies for infant baptism

There are two problems here—sponsors and the language of efficacy. The sponsors should be viewed as proxies speaking on behalf of one who cannot speak for himself—his obligations are voiced through their mouths. From this point of view it does not matter who speaks the obligations—it is simply that from a formal point of view (and liturgy has a formal character) the obligation to believe in Jesus and to walk in newness of life is expressed by the infant candidate as it would be by the adult. Infant baptism carries the same obligations as adult—and a parent who believes that God does in fact require this Christian way of life from his child from earliest days will not shrink from having the obligation expressed as belonging to the child.[1] The other problem is 'seeing that this child is regenerate' etc. Here we can but turn to the language of scripture again, as set out on page 7 above. If baptism is to *initiate,* then in formal terms the candidate comes unregenerate and unforgiven, and is regenerated in baptism and declared to be so. Formal rites must take this form, or they become useless. It *may* be (and this is open to argument) that the theology expressed is inappropriate to particular persons who come as candidates, but this is an argument against the candidature *not* against using the New Testament language of baptismal efficacy in a baptismal service[2]. The problem probably originates from being unwilling to use the language of efficacy over *adults.* And this unwillingness probably arises from delaying baptism for adults. But if we returned to the practice of the Day of Pentecost or of Paul with the Philippian jailer, then we should feel that the language of efficacy is totally appropriate. And by retracing the argument, we should be willing to use it for infants also. If we are to treat persons as unregenerate until they are baptised, and as regenerate thereafter, then we should not be afraid to use this sort of language at the baptism.[3]

2. Indiscriminate Baptism

The only case made above is for the baptism of the child of a believer or of believers. To go on from this to the baptism of every newborn Englishman or Englishwoman is not only to take the case beyond where it can properly go, it is also to make it incredible. And the problem to-day is that the Baptist is so accustomed to the indiscriminate *practice* of infant baptism,

---

[1] Of course there are pedobaptists who do not ask these questions of the child, but instead ask the parents how they will bring the child up. This is less satisfactory, as it suggests that adult baptism carries obligations, and that infant baptism does not (contrary to Romans 6)—or at least they are not expressed. This is a peripheral point to the very propriety of baptising infants. But it can be seen that the Anglican approach here has a certain theological consistency.

[2] An instance which is not exactly parallel, but may be illustrative, is provided by the categorical language we use in marriage. If on occasion a bigamist goes through the service and is still pronounced to be truly married thereby (although there are unknown factors which are preventing it being a true marriage), that is an argument for scrutinising the candidates better, *not* for introducing a whole series of 'ifs' and 'buts' into the liturgy. See my discussion in Booklet no. 65, *Liturgy for Initiation.*

[3] The language used at the Lord's Supper provides a very close parallel.

that he is unable within it to see the New Testament *theology* of infant baptism (which would not justify the current abuses). Those who argue for widespread pedobaptism on grounds of sentiment, or history, or evangelistic opportunity, actually damage their own case till it cannot be sustained.[1]

To the Baptist we would say 'Please see that it is only a narrow case we are making, and please examine *that* on its merits.' To the indiscriminate baptiser of infants we would say 'Please see that you are making it impossible for many good Christians to understand what infant baptism is all about, and are unnecessarily polarising Christians for an illusory gain.'

3. What of 're-baptism'?
No-one actually believes in re-baptism. But many say that an infant baptism is no baptism, and many converted in later years, and under strong pressure of various sorts, are tempted to renounce their apparently useless infant baptism as no baptism, and have another baptism. It is my hope that this booklet will have suggested to them, firstly that infant baptism is true baptism, secondly that to say any baptism is not baptism is to run the risk of renouncing later even an adult baptism (as having been imperfectly understood or forgotten or something), thirdly that opinions ought to be formed about how *Christians* should bring up their children before the use of infant baptism is understood, and fourthly that there is a difference between the genuine objective validity and the more variable subjective efficacy. Thus a baptised person can value the appeals in Scripture to the *meaning of being a baptised person,* even if he or she found that conversion and faith in fact only followed at a long time after baptism.

4. Mode
It is traditional in discussion with a Baptist for the pedobaptist to find that the other is oscillating from discussing the age of baptism to discussing the mode. The main plea here is that they are totally separable subjects and should not be confused (one can for instance be a submerging pedobaptist or an affusing Baptist, as the first English Baptists were, so I understand). The subsidiary plea is that pouring water is sufficient for baptism, and, for what it is worth, this is probably what was done to the 3,000 on the Day of Pentecost, the Philippian Jailer, etc. It is what had to be done for the first forty years of missionary work in the Arctic. It may be argued that submersion is appropriate, and even preferable, but it cannot be shown that it is requisite. Thus infant baptism, though usually conducted by pouring water rather than by submerging the candidate, ought not to be rejected on those grounds.

5. Confirmation
This is not the place to argue in general about confirmation. All we ask is that no arguments for pedobaptism should be made to rest upon the existence of a later rite, confirmation. The argument must be *from* infant baptism *to* confirmation, and not the other way round. One might add here that the arguments above do not assume even the existence of a rite called confirmation. It may be advisable to go on from infant baptism to a later ratification of vows, but such advice is no part of the case here offered.

[1] For a fuller discussion of this see my booklet no. 98 in this series, *Policies for Infant Baptism.*

9. CONCLUSION

Such is the case. Infant baptism fits the evidence far better than any other conclusion. The case rests.

POSTSCRIPT

I used Postscripts in the second and third editions to introduce factors subsequent to the publication of the first edition of this Booklet in 1973. The main one was the strong reaction of David Pawson, whom I asked to write a measured reply and added my own answer to him, and the two pieces were published together in no. 24, *Infant Baptism under Cross-Examination.* I have since then endeavoured to keep no. 24 in print alongside this original 'Case'.[1]

I also mentioned in previous Postscripts a book by Donald Bridge and David Phypers, *The Water that Divides: The Baptism Debate* (IVP, 1977). Coming from the IVP, this weighty and scholarly book was almost by definition bound to keep a balance between pedobaptists and Baptist positions. Some Grove Booklets are mentioned in its bibliography, but none are cited in the text. The authors have taken little heed of the force of the following arguments which I have aired in this present Booklet:

1. The meaning of 'faith' in a new-born infant (as, e.g. on page 27).
2. The re-handling of the 'covenant' argument here (on pages 9-12).
3. The ecclesiological argument about the status of the unbaptised (as, e.g. on pages 16-19).
4. The argument about the giving of baptism *at the beginning of the Christian life* (as, e.g. on pages 15-16).

The incorporation of these matters into their discussion should certainly have brought down the scales on the pedobaptist side.

The 1970s and 1980s have also seen in England the rise firstly of the charismatic movement within the historic Churches (and particularly in the Church of England), and then of the 'house-churches' (or the Restorationists) far outside the historic Churches, exercising a strong pull on individuals to secede from them. Whilst charismatics, with an emphasis upon the immediacy of experiential religion, inevitably have a tendency to want the experience of adult baptism (probably by submersion), irrespective of whether they earlier had infant baptism or not, the house-churches are almost invariably wholly Baptist in their stance. Thus the pressures upon Anglicans and others to abandon hard thought on the issue and to go with the baptismal tide have been very strong. I have written a little in the latest edition of no. 61, *One Baptism Once*, and elsewhere about the possibility of renewing baptismal vows *in water*, but the main response must be a trenchant defence of pedobaptistsm.

On the other hand we now have the two books by Anglican evangelicals mentioned on page 2. We also have, in Mark Dalby's *Open Baptism* (S.P.C.K., 1989) a chapter headed 'Where Grove Goes Wrong' *(sic)*. Whilst this is directed specifically at baptismal *policies* – and is attempting to reverse history to a point fifty years ago - clearly this present Booklet is included in the sweeping condemnation. Let the reader decide. For myself, I see little of wrestling with the scriptures in his book (except Mark 10, of course), and much that makes the argument with Baptists, to which the present Booklet is devoted, a hundred times more difficult.

---

[1] David Pawson has written his own book, *The Normal Christian Birth* (Hodder and Stoughton, 1989), **but** the baptism of infants is relegated to a brief Liturgical (and fairly dismissive) appendix.